Presented to:

••

••

Never Forget The Difference You've Made

Made in the USA
Las Vegas, NV
03 August 2023

75615259R00059